Poems for the Heart

With Steps to Grow By

Cheryl L. Nicks

Photos by Cheryl L. Nicks

Heart Tones Publishing

New Orleans, Louisiana

Heart Tones Publishing
© 2010 by Cheryl L. Nicks

Library Of Congress Cataloguing-In-Publication Data

Nicks, Cheryl L.

Poems for the Heart With Steps to Grow By /

Cheryl L. Nicks

ISBN 145381616X
EAN-13 9781453816165

1. Poetry.

Printed in the United States of America

10 9 8 7 6 5 4 3 2 1

First edition

Photo Credits: Unless otherwise credited,
all photos are from the author's collection.

I dedicate this book to my Mother Dear,
Mrs. Girlie L. Nicks.

You inspired me to complete my first
(with many more to come)
book of poetry.

I LOVE YOU.

Dear Mother,

I wrote a version of your poem,
Profile of a Woman.

Since you couldn't find the original,
I wrote mine as a tribute
to the woman I've always known you to be.

Profile of a Woman

Dear Mother, you wrote that poem over 50 years ago;

The words you no longer know.

You passed your love of poetry to me through my DNA,

Mother please hear what I have to say.

Your childhood was filed with struggle and strife,

You've had such a hard life.

At a very young age you had five little ones—

Three daughters and two sons.

You never drank or smoked;

To your children you were always yoked.

I loved the way you combed my hair.

You kept us clean, even when the cupboards were bare.

You pinched pennies so that we could eat.

Many nights, your stomach empty, you went to sleep.

You had to walk me two miles to and from school,

Whether it was hot, whether it was cool.

You wanted us to have more than you had.

When you couldn't buy us things, it made you sad.

You took care of other people's children too

Because that's what a real woman would do.

You encouraged us to get an education;

You knew that would be our salvation.

When I look in the mirror, I see parts of you.

I'm a beautiful, loving, giving woman because of you.

Mother Dear I often smile;

I'm so proud to carry Your Profile.

Cheryl L. Nicks and book writing mentor, Mark Victor Hansen, creator of the *Chicken Soup for the Soul* series.

Gratitude

I thank my three daughters, Raynika R. Broussard, Tia L. Broussard and Laci P. Broussard for always encouraging me to do whatever makes me happy;

Brother Suave R. Walker for coaching me with a "Just do *you*" mantra;

Dan Smith for challenging me to write this book of poetry after hearing my poems;

Tawana Williams for encouraging me to follow my passion;

Evelyn Polk for being my cheerleader;

Sharon LeBoeuf, my dear friend who was always willing to switch workdays so that I could attend my workshops and coaching;

Carey Ann Strelecki, my editor and Meaghan Boeing, my graphic designer, for going above and beyond the call of duty;

Star Bobatoon and Wade Randolph for their masterminds; and

Valorie N. Parker for allowing me to be guest speaker and present my poems on her "Hot Topics from the Soul" talk show.

Introduction

During a conversation with my mother, age 73, she surprised me by telling me that as a young woman she also loved reading and writing inspirational poetry. She said that she'd even written a poem about herself called "Profile of a Woman," but she could no longer remember it. My mother was doing 50 years ago what I'm passionately doing now. At that moment, I understood my gift of poetry.

A few months before I wrote this book, I contracted a virus that attacked my brain, which could have caused brain damage, paralysis, or death. And as I was lying in the emergency room, with a headache that morphine wasn't relieving, I thought about the books I'd never written and the CDs I'd never produced. That was a wake-up call for me. Thankfully, I made a speedy recovery and I knew that I needed to share my poetry with the world.

The graveyard is the richest place on Earth
Because most people never fulfill their dreams after their birth.
We keep putting them off until tomorrow;
We reach old age and look back in sorrow.
Many people stand over us crying when we've come to our end,
Not only because we're gone,
But because our books and music are still within.

What legacy will you leave on the planet?

I invite you to stop living like you have a thousand years.

Cheryl L. Nicks

Table of Contents

Introduction i

What Love Is..1

Just Be 3

The Tao of The Now...5

A Stranger Touched Me Today...7

The Power To Choose 9

Emotional Bus 11

Only Positive People..13

The Beauty of Relationship 15

Your Past Doesn't Equal Your Future 17

Fingerprints 19

How to Find Love...21

To Thy Own Self Be True 23

True Friend...25

Sunshine...27

The Book of Life...29

What Love Is

Love is a quality of one's heart.
If we fully understood that, we'd be so smart.
Love isn't something that you can find;
It's something that's within us all of the time.
Many expect someone to give it to them;
No one can give what's already within.
Love is a basic human need;
It's not authentic if you have to beg and plead.
For so many, trying to get love is a must,
But what we give will surely come back to us.
Love is what keeps our hearts warm.
Love is the calm after the storm.
Only when we love ourselves can we connect to another.
Love that comes from the heart is like no other.

Steps to Grow By

Learn to love yourself first.
Going around this step
Will only make matters worse.
Cultivate the love that's within;
It will truly make your heart grin.
Accept yourself, love yourself, and live.
Love isn't something you get,
Love is something you give.

Just Be

When you look around and all that you see
And most of what you hear is negativity,
Sit still and just be!

When the weight of the world is dragging you down,
When your usual smile has turned to a frown,
Take some deep breaths, just be!

When you're flying high on cloud nine,
When your day is full of bright sunshine,
Open your heart and just be!

When you know that you've done your best
And now it's time for much needed rest,
Close your eyes and just be!

Steps to Grow By

Take a pause from the need to do
Or the hundreds of things to pursue.
Gaze upon the tallest tree,

Experience stillness, just be!

The Tao of The Now

Some people say that they have to make time.
How dare the Ego give that thought to the mind!
Do we honestly believe that we possess the power
To create a second, minute, or an hour?
The only real time is right now.
The mind can't grasp that, it keeps asking how.
As you stand here, the future you seek.
The future is today, right now, not next week.
When you remember the past, you do so now.
These concepts are part of the Tao of the now.

Steps to Grow By

Believing that you are your past is just a delusion.
Believing that you can control the past is also an illusion.
Let go of the past, you're not there, you're here.
May you learn to live in the present without fear.

A Stranger Touched Me Today

Driving down the street one bright sunny day,
An elderly lady standing on a corner looked my way.
I thought maybe she needed a ride, so I circled back around.
She said thank you, I prayed for an angel to take me to town.
She shared life stories, said that she was 81.
We laughed, talked, I still remember the song she sung.
I thought how this beautiful stranger really touched my heart
And how that ride to town was far too short.
I arrived home thankful that our eyes had met.
I'll cherish that experience and that lady I'll never forget.

Steps to Grow By

Ask yourself each morning, to whom can I be of service today?
You never know who the universe will send your way.
Give a stranger a smile, that's all some really yearn,
And you will truly be touched when you receive one in return.

The Power To Choose

We all have a gift, that's the power to choose.
If we use it wisely, we can't lose.
That gift set us way above the animal species,
But choices are not always met with ease.
Our choices can create the life we desire.
In the midst of adversity, we can walk through the fire.
Just know that you always have a choice.
Don't be silent, you *can* lift your voice.
Even in your darkest hour,
Remember that gift of choice—now that's power!

Steps to Grow By

Ignore the statement "you don't have a choice."
When you are relentless your actions match your voice.
Stand up for yourself, don't slumber, don't snooze.
Use your gift, the power to choose.

Emotional Bus

What's really driving *your* bus?
Most times we believe that it is us.
What emotions occupy your seats?
What limiting rituals do you constantly repeat?
Are your seats filled with guilt, I'm not good enough, or hurt?
You can refill them with love, value and self worth.
As your bus rolls lovingly down the street,
What other positive emotions will you put in your seats?

Steps to Grow By

If your bus is filled with pity, fear, and shame,
Step off, you can't see the picture when you're in the frame.
Say, "Today *I* will choose how I want to feel…
Only positive emotions and I won't break that deal."
Of the hundreds of emotions available to us
Only a handful *truly* drive our bus.

Only Positive People

Other people's attitude can negatively affect your day
If you sit around and listen to negative things they say.
That saying, attitudes are contagious, is true.
Pay attention to how words affect you.
If your energy doesn't match, don't stay in your seat.
Your life accomplishments are a result of the company that you keep.
The perpetual optimist is who you should be;
From the perpetual pessimist you must flee.

Steps to Grow By

Seek out people who are going where you want to go;
They will help you with what you need to know.
Only positive people you should surround.
Because if people can't bring you up,
Please don't let them bring you down.

The Beauty of Relationship

You're floating on a cloud when you find Ms. or Mr. Right.
Then the mask comes off and the day turns to night.
Why did you enter into relationship, do you even know?
Were you wanting someone to make you feel good or were you wanting to grow?
Relationships brings to surface some of our deepest fears:
Will he/she love me, leave me, or can we stay together for years?
You have to be all that you want the other person to be,
Because when you look in the mirror it will be you that you see.
Then the eyes will connect to the heart;
That connection will be felt, even when you're apart.
During the good times and bad, the struggles and strife,
You'll know that you've come together to *enhance each other's life.*

Steps to Grow By

When relationships take a downward turn,
Ask yourself, *what lessons have I learned?*
Don't beat yourself up or wish you'd stayed longer.
Each relationship should make you stronger.
Cherish the good, and here's a tip:
All of that is the Beauty of Relationship.

Your Past Doesn't Equal Your Future

In search of our identity, sometimes we go back far.
But where we come from isn't necessarily who we are.
Knowing where you've been shapes what you believe.
It's best to focus on where you're going and what you can achieve.
The things you focus on will expand.
When others see you moving forward, they'll lend a helping a hand.
No matter the circumstances of your past,
Into the future you decide what to cast.
But if it doesn't serve you, let it stay back,
Because right now you're on the fast track.

Steps to Grow By

I invite you to say, "Today I let go
Of any experience that won't help me to grow.
I will look to my past only if it builds me up.
I'm moving forward and that I won't disrupt."
Be thankful for all that you've been through;
All of it has had a part in shaping you.

Fingerprints

Our fingerprints are uniquely ours.
Look at your hands and observe the spirals.
Have you ever thought "WOW, this is my identity;
These tiny lines and curves can really ID me?"
Think of all of the things you've touched throughout your life.
Did you leave prints of love or heartache and strife?
What about the people, your path did cross?
Some were only acquaintances, some may have been your boss;
Some stayed a short while, only for a season,
But they all were drawn to you for a special reason.
There are some from your mind, will never depart
Because they came into your life and left their fingerprints on your heart.

Steps to Grow By

Look for a lesson from those who come your way.
Everyone you meet isn't meant to stay.
Whether good or bad someone touched you;
Always remember that *you* leave fingerprints too.

How to Find Love

Our basic human need for love is so strong,
Some search for it their whole life long.
Look, is love over there?
Are you trying to find love everywhere?
Many say I'll find love if I only sit and wait;
Others say I'll find love no matter what it takes.
Love has always been and is inside of you.
Love isn't something you find, love is something you do.

Steps to Grow By

Put out into the Universe what you want to come back to you.
The Law of Reciprocity really is true.
Be giving and authentic in all that you do;
You won't have to find love, *Love will find you.*

To Thy Own Self Be True

I'd like you to answer the question, "Who are you?"
Do you really know, *do you?*
You're a policeman, a therapist, or a preacher;
You're a nurse, a mommy, a Sunday school teacher.
How can you to yourself be true
When you can't separate who you are from what you do?
So first, to thy own self be true,
Because the whole world is awaiting you.
When you can say, "I truly know me,"
You will be an example, the Universe will see.

Steps to Grow By

Your job isn't who you are.
To find that answer go deep inside, *really far.*
Meet your character, value, and heart.
Yes that's a great place to start!!!

True Friend

People come into your life for a day or a season,
But a true friend comes and stays for a reason.
They're someone you can talk to, someone in whom to confide,
Someone you can complain to when your last nerve has been tried.
A true friend won't judge you or talk behind your back,
Because they understand that sacred pact.
They encourage you to continue to grow;
They will be honest when you ask "should I let go?"
Even when they see some crazy things you do,
They will continue to stand by you.
When you call them because you've had a scare,
You know that they'll be there. You know how much they care.

Steps to Grow By

Look at all of the people who always need you.
Look closer at the ones around when you need someone too.
When you're down on your luck, many leave as fast as the wind;
The ones who stay are your *true* friends.

Sunshine

The sun is always shining above the clouds.
I'd heard that saying, but didn't understand how.
I'd flown hundreds of times, sat by the window,
Amazed at how fast airplanes really go.
One day I had my ticket to board the plane.
'It is storming, the sky is very dark, I must be insane.'
With boarding pass in hand, all blood has left my feet;
With fear and reservation, I take my seat.
We took off through that terrible storm;
I'm hoping that my feet will soon warm.
We rose above the clouds, and to my surprise,
The most beautiful sunshine met my eyes,
And the bluest sky I had ever seen.
Now I know what that saying means.

Steps to Grow By

When your life is cloudy and you can't see the sky,
May you look at problems with a different eye.
You have to go on but don't know how;
Just remember the sun is always shinning above the clouds.

The Book of Life

Life is a journey with lessons to be learned;
With each new day, a different page is turned.
Each chapter is filled with twists and turns, ups and downs,
Breathtaking beautiful scenery, all ranges of lovely sounds.
What things have you put on the pages of your book?
Were there good deeds, would you be proud if people looked?
Did you waste time, your dreams not pursue?
Did you judge people because they were different from you?
Or did you serve others and try to stay true?
When your book of life is closed, what will people say about you?

Steps to Grow By

Learn something every day no matter how small.
Be of service to others, answer the call.
Even when you don't realize it, in your book you write,
And it all stays in *your* Book of Life!

About the Author

Cheryl L. Nicks was born and raised in New Orleans, Louisiana. For the first 13 years of her life, she and her family lived with her maternal grandmother. She was the first grandchild and the apple of her grandmother's eye.

Her childhood was filled with poverty and adversity, but she saw the strength of her mother and grandmother, and watched as they used their religious faith to carry them through adversity.

Cheryl periodically wrote poems to escape the reality of her environment. After attaining her dream of becoming a registered nurse, she put her poetry on a shelf and only wrote sporadically.

She has always had a passion for our nation's youth. After listening to a Les Brown CD, she was inspired to pursue speaking to youth all around the country. Cheryl's coaching with Les Brown, her passion for poetry and our youth, and a heartfelt conversation with her mother all came together and enlightened her to her purpose: writing and reciting poems that touch the mind, body, and heart, which in turn leads to healing, growth, and a better YOU!

Cheryl L. Nicks is also a:
Board Certified Nurse Practitioner,
Certified Gestalt Psychotherapist,
Certified Professional Life Coach,
President of Nicks International Community Foundation,
Producer, recording artist, and owner of MoYo Entertainment Inc.

Other books
co-authored by Cheryl L. Nicks:

Meeting Les Brown, Ms Mammie Brown's Baby Boy

and

Fight for Your Dreams,
a forthcoming e-book with Les Brown

Poems for the Heart with Steps to Grow By is also available on CD.

8531379R0

Made in the USA
Charleston, SC
18 June 2011